Lexicon of Intentionally Ambiguous Recommendations (LIAR)

Robert Thornton

Meadowbrook
Distributed by Simon & Schuster
New York, New York

Library of Congress
Cataloging-in-Publication Data
THORNTON, ROBERT
LEXICON OF INTENTIONALLY
AMBIGUOUS RECOMMENDATIONS
(LIAR) / ROBERT THORNTON.
1. EMPLOYMENT REFERENCES—UNITED
STATES.
2. EMPLOYMENT REFERENCES. I. TITLE.
HF5549.5.R45T46 1988 650.1'4—DC19
ISBN 0-88166-111-2

Cover Illustration by Mike Reed
Edited by Patricia McKernon

Published by Meadowbrook, Inc.
18318 Minnetonka Boulevard
Deephaven, MN 55391

BOOK TRADE DISTRIBUTION
by Simon & Schuster
a division of
Simon & Schuster Inc.
1230 Avenue of the Americas
New York, NY 10020

S&S Ordering #: 0-671-66401-8

88 89 90 91 10 9 8 7 6 5 4 3 2 1

Printed in the United States of America

·DEDICATION·

To my family

·ACKNOWLEDGMENTS·

I owe a debt of gratitude to many people for their generous assistance in the preparation of this book. Special thanks goes to Eli Schwartz—who spawned the first LIAR phrase—and to Bill Johnson, whose timely press release generated widespread interest in the collection. I am also grateful to many other Lehigh University colleagues for their help and suggestions: Jim Hobbs, Ken Sinclair, Jon Innes, Bruce Smackey, Steve Thode, Tom and Jean Hyclak, George Beezer, Diane Oechsle, Rene Hollinger, Dick Barsness, Mike Kolchin, Ray Horton, Nicholas Balabkins, David Leahigh, Christy Roysdon, and George Nation.

Many friends and colleagues outside of Lehigh also provided me with helpful ideas, among them Malcolm Rees, Charles Moyer, David Greenaway, Harry Dower, Mike Hodges, Dan Ramsdell, and Ray Larson. I am indebted to Peter How and Clark Kerr for allowing me to use several of their own ambiguous gems.

Special thanks (better yet, sympathy) is due to members of my family who were forced to listen to or read through numerous (yawn!) versions of the manuscript: Julie Thornton, Jenni Thornton, Bobby Thornton, and (when *no one* else could take any more) Muffy Thornton. I would also like to thank Kathy Fergus, Kathy Wadington, Mary Beth Balcarcel, Dorothy Menze, Denise Roske, Ann and Frank Roske, and Mary Thornton.

Finally, I am most grateful to Bruce Lansky for his enthusiasm, advice, and support and to Patricia McKernon for her careful editing. Patricia also taught me that the boundaries of equal opportunity are much wider than I would ever have imagined.

For the assistance of all of these people, no amount of thanks will suffice.

Contents

....

Introduction
····

Have you ever been asked by someone to write a letter of recommendation? You probably have. But have you ever written an *unfavorable* letter about someone? Be honest, now—I bet you haven't. Most likely it's not because you've only been approached by persons of such superior talents and work habits that you just couldn't say anything negative. No, chances are you—like most of us—have difficulty writing anything bad about a person whom you may have worked closely with, lived next door to, or had in class. Even if that person is totally incompetent, you probably hem, haw, waffle, gnash your teeth ... and then wind up writing a very favorable letter—all the while berating yourself for being a wimp.

But don't be too hard on yourself. It's much more difficult nowadays to write an honest letter of recommendation when your words may not be confidential. Today, a person can exercise a legal right to read your letter—and even sue if the contents are not to his or her liking and are insufficiently substantiated.

Wouldn't it be nice if you could convey unfavorable information about someone without having that person perceive or prove it as such? Well weep, worry, waffle, and gnash no more. The *Lexicon of Intentionally Ambiguous Recommendations*, or *LIAR* for short, has been designed expressly for this purpose. The lexicon is a collection of phrases and sentences that offer both a negative *and* positive opinion of a candidate's personal qualities, work habits, motivation, etc. For example, to describe someone who is woefully inept, you could say:

> "I recommend this candidate with no qualifications whatsoever."

> or

> "I simply can't say enough good things about him."

The candidate can take these statements as high praise, the reader of the recommendation can be tipped off, and you can get off the hook.

This volume contains several hundred such humorous sentences and phrases. For the letter-writer's convenience, the various lexicon entries are grouped by undesirable traits such as absenteeism, alcohol/drug problems, incompetence, loose moral character, and stupidity.

In addition to the collection of sentences and phrases, *LIAR* contains a brief discussion of the legal controversy surrounding letters of recommendation today (chapter one). There is also a guide (chapter two) for the do-it-yourselfer who wants to learn how to develop original phrases. The guide shows how to dangle participles, mutilate punctuation marks (painlessly), and create havoc with deliberate typographical errors. For the busy professional, there is even a chapter (chapter four) of form letters of recommendation. All are certifiably ambiguous, litigation-proof, and ready-to-go. Just pop in a name and sign it. Finally, the book contains a chapter on how to give ambiguous oral recommendations. The telephone recommendation, in particular, is preferred by many people today because it leaves fewer traces—an important consideration in today's litigious atmosphere.

This book is expanded from an article I wrote entitled " 'I Can't Recommend the Candidate Too Highly': An Ambiguous Lexicon for Job Recommendations," which was first published in the *Chronicle of Higher Education*.[1]

Ready with your sense of humor? Tongue in cheek? Then let's take off!

---

[1]Robert J. Thornton, " 'I Can't Recommend the Candidate Too Highly': An Ambiguous Lexicon for Job Recommendations," *Chronicle of Higher Education*, February 25, 1987, p. 42.

The Legal Context
····

·THE BIG SWEAT·

You work for a major corporation and you've just been asked to write a letter of recommendation for a co-worker who wants a top management job at another firm. The problem is, you've worked with this fellow long enough to know that he can't manage his own sock drawer. What do you say? Do you tell him you don't think he's suitable for the position and that you can't give him a recommendation? (Remember, if he doesn't get the job, you have to continue working with him.) Or do you agree to write the recommendation and lie to the prospective employer about his qualifications?

You're a college professor and, after a knock on your office door, in walks a student asking for a letter of recommendation for a job. Do you remember the student? Of course you do. She's the one who wrote on her examination paper in World History that Louis XIV was "King of the Sun," and chastised Martin Luther for nailing ninety-five theologians to a church door.[1] But the student has a pleasing personality—even if her view of history is somewhat warped—and also happens to be the dean's daughter. What do you do?

You're at home relaxing on your porch one evening, and your neighbor stops by to ask if you would agree to act as a character reference for him. Character reference, you think to yourself. This guy's a character, all right. He's burned down his garage shooting off illegal fireworks, is loaded five nights a week, and once used inflated condoms instead of balloons at his daughter's birthday party (the stores were all closed). What do you say to him?

In any of these cases, you would probably write a favorable letter even when you know the candidate is mediocre or unqualified. Why? For several reasons. Many people (I among them) suffer from the "marshmallow syndrome," a chronic affliction that causes people to break out in a cold sweat, bite their nails, and lose sleep when they have to make a frank—but unfavorable—evaluation of another person. The problem has become far more widespread in the last few years because more and more candidates are now exercising their legal right to read letters of recommendation. Many people are pursuing litigation if the contents are not to their liking and are poorly documented.

---

[1] Anders Henriksson, "A History of the Past: 'Life Reeked with Joy,' " *Wilson Quarterly* (Spring 1983), pp. 168-171.

·LITIGATION?·

You bet. Consider the following cases:

Larry Buck was fired by his employer for allegedly missing sales targets. When he couldn't get work with other firms, he hired a detective to sniff out the recommendation given him by his former employer. The detective found out that the former employer was referring to him as a "Jekyll and Hyde person, a classic sociopath." Buck went on to sue his former employer for malicious slander and was awarded nearly $2 million.

Joseph Beale was fired from his job as a tugboat captain because he refused to cross a picket line in a labor dispute. When asked by prospective employers to evaluate Beale's work, his former employer replied that he was fired for "mutiny." Beale sued, and the court socked his former employer with punitive damages for malice.[2]

Joe Schmoe (an alias) quit his management job at a bank after refusing to take a lie-detector test as part of an inquiry into missing bank funds. Later, he had difficulty finding other work in the banking field and filed a $1.25 million suit against his former employer for giving a bad reference.[3]

---

[2]The first two examples summarized here are discussed in more detail in "The Revenge of the Fired," *Newsweek*, 16 February, 1987, pp. 46-7.

[3]Robert Douglas, "Lawsuits Are Putting a Chill on Bad Job References," *Allentown Morning Call*, 22 June 1987, p. B11.

In a nutshell, letters of recommendation are no longer confidential. What's more, people on the receiving end of unfavorable letters of recommendation are increasingly apt to sue—successfully, too. According to Jury Verdict Research, over the last seven years employees in the State of California have won 72 percent of all job-related lawsuits, with the average settlement running over $500,000.[4]

What's happening as a result? More and more firms are unwilling to provide prospective employers of former workers with any more information than "name, rank, and serial number." In other words, they simply verify the fact that the person once worked there, in this or that capacity, for so long a period. Increasingly, employment consultants are advising firms to clam up on recommendations. According to James Challenger, president of the outplacement firm of Challenger, Gray and Christmas, "We are advising our clients to give out nothing but basic information on former employees."[5]

Maybe this is all right, you might say. Perhaps letters of recommendation should be abolished as a requirement of employment. I don't think so. The fact remains that firms simply have no *potentially* better means of gaining reliable information about a candidate's qualifications than through people who have had close contact with him or her. Even firms that refuse to provide letters of recommendation for

---

[4]Forrest S. Gossett, "On References, There's One Key Policy," *Allentown Morning Call*, 1 June 1987, p. B9.
[5]Ibid.

their own former employees apparently believe this. For at the same time that they refuse to give information about former employees, they often continue to require and check references of those whom they do employ.[6] It's in their interests to do so because they're being squeezed by litigation from current employees as well.

For example, one employee who was assaulted by a janitor successfully sued the firm for not researching the janitor's background more thoroughly before hiring him. In another recent case, a woman sued an airline because she was bitten by a boarding agent (yes, he was a human) who was trying to stop her from entering a plane. The agent turned out to have AIDS. In her suit, the woman claimed that the airline company should have known of the man's disease and propensity for violence.[7]

Because of cases like these, employers now find themselves between a rock and a hard place. Giving bad references often leads to lawsuits—so employers don't want to give references. But not seeking out references can also lead to lawsuits if some employees harm other employees or the public. What to do?

[6]"Reference Checking: What's the Point When Everyone Is Afraid to Talk?" *Wall Street Journal*, 5 May 1987, p. 1.

[7]Larry Reibstein, "Firms Face Lawsuits for Hiring People Who Commit Crimes," *Wall Street Journal*, 30 April 1987, p. 33.

·THE LEXICON·

Obviously, employers should be able to write recommendations without fear of lawsuits. They need a way to convey honest—though perhaps unfavorable—information about a candidate for a job *without the candidate being able to prove or even perceive it as such.* To this end, I have designed the Lexicon of Intentionally Ambiguous Recommendations—LIAR, for short. Two samples from the lexicon should illustrate the approach:

- *To describe a candidate who is not very industrious:* "In my opinion, you will be very fortunate to get this person to work for you."

- *To describe a candidate who is certain to foul up any project:* "I am sure that whatever task he undertakes—no matter how small—he will be fired with enthusiasm."

Phrases like these allow an evaluator to offer a negative opinion of the candidate's personal qualities, work habits, or motivation, yet enable the candidate to believe that he or she has been praised highly.

The phrases in the lexicon are not simply vague or ambiguous. Rather, they convey a double meaning that can be interpreted as either high praise or damning criticism. In this way, they satisfy everyone. The writer can sleep without feeling guilty about having compromised his or her principles ("I told it like it was ... well, almost.") *and* without fear of being slapped with a lawsuit. The person for whom the recommendation was written is at best pleased ("Gee, Harry wrote me a very nice letter.") or at worst perplexed ("Just what *did* he mean by saying I will be 'fired with enthusiasm'?"). And the recipient of the letter? How is he or she to interpret the ambiguous recommendation? Any way at all!

The
LIAR Guide

····

·GETTING STARTED·

Maybe now you're convinced of the potential value of ambiguous letters of recommendation. But are they easy to write? Well, with a little assistance and a bit of practice, you'll find that they are.

In this chapter you will learn some tricks to the art—or more appropriately *craft*—of writing ambiguously. For although the lexicon in the next chapter is large, many more undiscovered ambiguous references probably exist out there in the vast verbal universe. And with a bit of practice dangling participles, mutilating punctuation marks, and executing typographical errors, soon you'll be crafting your own ambiguous recommendations.

You'll learn three ways to write ambiguously. You can mess up the syntax, or structure, of a sentence. You can punctuate it obscurely. Or you can intentionally make confusing typos. I'll walk you through each device and explain carefully how to create maximum confusion.

·SYNTACTICAL AMBIGUITY·

If you remember your high school English class, you will recall Miss Grundy warning you of the dangers of misplaced modifiers—particularly dangling participles. (As a young boy, I thought that dangling a participle was a mortal sin.) Dangling participles are modifiers that seem to refer to two different words or to a word that isn't even in the sentence. As such, they can be used to create double meanings. Consider this one:

"The volume of work which Mr. Smith performs, while staggering, is only a fraction of what he is capable of doing."

The participle *staggering*, in this sentence, is dangling. The reader is not sure just who or what is staggering here—Mr. Smith (who may enjoy an occasional nip on the job) or the workload that he handles.

Here's another example:

"He had a lot of brass pushing for his promotion."

The misplaced modifier *pushing*—again a participle—could either be construed as modifying *brass* (meaning that his promotion had the support of the bigwigs upstairs) or *he* (which would turn a flattering statement into a negative one).

Misplacing modifiers is not so hard to do, but getting your participles to dangle *ambiguously* is difficult. Miss Grundy was a tough cookie, and reversing learned behavior is not easy. You may be comforted to know that the ability to dangle participles is not genetically inherited. It simply requires practice. Therefore, the person who aspires to create ambiguous phrases is encouraged to engage in regular dangling exercises—five per day to start, working up to twenty per day. Sometimes it helps to dangle them with a friend.

·AMBIGUOUS PUNCTUATION·

·The Quomma·

A wide variety of ambiguous recommendations can be written using a little known (as yet) punctuation mark called a "questionable comma"—or "quomma" for short. It looks like a comma but also could be mistaken for, say, a small coffee stain, a defect in the paper, or maybe even a dead gnat or fruitfly. The quomma takes many forms, but often looks like this: ,

... or like this: ,

... or like this: ,

You get the idea. The reader thinks it might be a comma, but can't be sure if it really is a comma or something else entirely.

In what types of situations is the quomma valuable? It's especially handy whenever a phrase or sentence would have one meaning if the mark is really a comma and another meaning if it is not.

This is all very theoretical, so let's use a few examples. Suppose the writer of a recommendation wishes to make an ambiguous statement about a lazy person in whom he or she has little confidence. The writer could state in a letter:

"He won't do anything which will lower your high regard for him."

Read without internal punctuation, the sentence seems to convey high praise, and indicates that the candidate's performance will very likely live up to his prospective employer's expectations. However, if a comma is inserted between the words *anything* and *which*, the sentence becomes:

"He won't do anything, which will lower your high regard for him."

The comma has changed a sentence of high praise to one of damning criticism.

Herein lies the utility of the quomma: it renders the sentence ambiguous. If a quomma is inserted between two critical words, the reader of the recommendation cannot tell whether it is truly a comma or not, and can interpret the sentence positively or negatively.

You might wonder why I've been so vague about the exact appearance or shape of the quomma. The reason is this: to be useful, the quomma must cause confusion as to whether it is or is not a comma. This is particularly true when quommas must be used in tandem, as in the following sentence:

"Her record speaks well of her." *[High praise]*

or

"Her record speaks, well, of her." *[A "nothing" comment]*

Clearly, using two quommas so close together would cause suspicion if they assumed the same shape.

Therefore, for those recommendations that use the quomma, I will simply use the letter o to indicate appropriate quomma placement, as in the following sentence:

"His credentials are nothing o which should be laughed at."

Not only does the o help the reader to recognize where this all-important punctuation mark must be placed, but it also makes the typesetter's work easier, since he has no quomma symbols and the press has a shortage of gnats and fruitflies.[1]

·The Schizocolon·

With a little imagination, you can use a semicolon to generate the same type of confusion as the quomma. For example, take the next sentence:

"Once he put his mind to a problem, he wouldn't stop until he had solved it."

Sounds like high praise? Just the type of employee you'd love to have working for you? Of course. But what if the comma after *problem* were a semicolon instead? Then the sentence would imply that most of the time the guy's mind was in low gear but that one time—just one time—he really did apply himself. In fact, this "schizophrenic semicolon" (or "schizocolon" for short) can be used effectively in a large number of sentences and phrases involving the word *once*. For example:

"Once he came to work; he was all business."

"Once he actually made a decision; he took great satisfaction from it."

"Once she gave up smoking; she was a much more productive employee."

---

[1]Helpful hint: Allowing a banana to age (gracefully) in your briefcase over a period of several months is one surefire way to allow the fruitfly population to (excuse me) be fruitful and multiply.

Writers who take delight in the schizocolon form it in various ways. Some have their secretaries actually type in the semicolon (and later blame the secretaries for the mistake). Others partially erase the upper half (the period) of the semicolon, leaving the reader to wonder which punctuation mark it really is. Still others apply a very small dollop of walnut-fudge topping for the upper half of the semicolon to cause maximum bewilderment. In the lexicon that follows, schizocolons will be noted with the symbol ⨟.

Quommas and schizocolons are not the only types of ambiguous punctuation marks in the lexicon. Sprinkled throughout, for example, you'll find "is-it-or-isn't-it hyphens." (I chose not to invent another cutesy term like 'quomma' for the is-it-or-isn't-it hyphen for fear we'd all start sounding like Elmer Fudd.) The creative user can fashion other types of ambiguous punctuation marks as the need arises.

·TYPO GOOFS·

A great many ambiguous phrases can result from deliberate typing slip-ups. "Typo goofs," as I call them, make the reader wonder if a typing error has occurred or if the sentence should be interpreted another way. Here are a few examples.

·Capital Confusion·

Can the misuse of capital and lowercase letters create ambiguity? Absolutely! This type of typo goof can be used to make the reader wonder whether the capital or lowercase form is appropriate for the initial letter of a word. For example, the writer of a recommendation might put in her letter:

> "He always shows a lot of Polish in his dealings with customers."

If the typist is careful to position the *p* in *polish* at a point a little above where a lowercase *p* should be and a little below where an uppercase *p* should be, then the reader of the recommendation will not be sure if the sentence means to say:

> The person in question is a smooth operator.

> or

> The person uses a kielbasa as a pointer in his demonstrations.

·The Space Oddity·

Another useful typo goof results from ambiguous spacing. For instance, a letter of recommendation might read:

> "Whenever there is a tough task at hand, this person is usually outstanding."

To render this phrase ambiguous, the typist should insert a half-space (or what I call a "space oddity") between the *t* and the *s* in *outstanding*. That way, the reader will be unsure whether the person handles pressure well, or—if the space is taken literally—perhaps whenever important work needs to be done the person is usually out standing somewhere else, maybe having a smoke.

In the lexicon (chapter three), words requiring the use of a space oddity will be written with a slash (/).

·NOW THEN...

After this little venture into grammatical deep space, you are ready to tackle the lexicon in the next chapter. Who knows? With a little practice you might one day receive the coveted Weasel Award—the LIAR enthusiast's equivalent of the black belt. In any case, becoming a master of the ambiguous letter of recommendation is virtually guaranteed to bring with it one further benefit: once your prowess is known, rarely will you be asked to write letters of recommendation. Come to think of it, I haven't been asked to write a single one since I wrote this book!

The Lexicon

••••

This chapter contains 250 ambiguous sentences and phrases you can use in letters of recommendation. Most of them convey opposite meanings—high praise or damning criticism. Some, however, are simply wishy-washy or what I call "nothing" recommendations. Their alternate meaning is not really bad, but rather ... well, not much of anything.

The lexicon covers fifteen categories of common employee problems:

        absenteeism
        alcohol/drug problems
        character defects
        criminal background
        disagreeableness
        dishonesty
        incompetence
        lack of ambition
        laziness
        loose morals
        mediocrity
        misfit
        stupidity
        unemployability
        unreliability

A final section contains recommendations for people with less common problems, such as vampirism or size 16E feet. (I can hear you snickering, but who knows when the need might arise for such a recommendation?)

Where appropriate, items will be footnoted to point out quommas, space oddities, schizocolons, or other devices for creating ambiguity. The footnotes will be especially useful for those lazy readers who did not do their homework and skipped over the LIAR guide (chapter two) before tackling the lexicon.

Absenteeism

· · · ·

Recommendation	Meaning
"A man like him is hard to find."	He disappears frequently.
"She's not your normal everyday employee."	... every *other* day, maybe.
"Once he came to work; he was all business."[1]	We never saw him again after that.
"When I knew her, it seemed that her career was just taking off."	...taking off for the shore, for the ball game, for the rest of the week ...

---

[1]For a discussion of the schizocolon (⸎), see pp. 22-23.

Alcohol/Drug Problems

· · · ·

Recommendation	Meaning
"The volume of work he performs, while staggering, is still only a fraction of what he can do."	Imagine how much he could do if he were sober.
"He often took a long time to write his reports, but that was because he usually had to go through several drafts before he thought everything sounded just right."	He works better with a couple of beers under his belt.
"She was always high in my opinion."	She was often seen smoking a joint.
"He works with as much speed as he can."	He's always popping uppers.

"We remember the hours he spent working with us as happy hours."

He was usually sloshed.

"She's a seasoned employee."

She's usually pickled, in fact.

"We generally found him loaded with work to do."

He'd usually get tanked before he'd work.

"I would say that his real talent is getting wasted at his current job."

He gets bombed regularly.

"He is a man of great visions."

He hallucinates.

"She is never tight with her money."

She prefers to get loaded on *other* people's dough.

"It won't take her long to get up to speed."

She does most other drugs already.

"If you want him to come to work for you, make sure there are no bars n the way."[2]

On the way, or *in* the way? If they're *on* the way, he's likely to stop in for a beer or two.

---

[2]The case of the vanishing letter. Just what is this word, anyway?

Character Defects
· · · ·

Recommendation	Meaning
"We often saw him l st in his work."[3]	Lost in his work? List in his work? Last in his work? Lust in his work?
"There is always a method to his madness."	He isn't *just* insane.
"I'd say that she may have been awed/odd by our firm's standards."[4]	She's a real weirdo.
"Most of us had rather good impressions of him."	...but there was this one guy who could mimic him perfectly.

---

[3]Ibid.
[4]This sentence uses a homophone and works for oral recommendations.
  For a discussion of homophones, see pp. 101-103.

"No matter what type of work you give her, I have no doubt that you will soon find her committed."

She's a certified nutcase and belongs in an institution.

"You'll be very impressed with his performance at work."

He's really quite a convincing actor.

"She gives every appearance of being a reliable, conscientious employee."

...but appearances are deceiving.

"He doesn't mind being disturbed."

He sees his shrink far less often than he should.

"He usually works in a frenzy."

The guy is manic.

Criminal Background

Recommendation	Meaning
"While he worked with us he was given numerous citations."	He was arrested many times.
"He's a man of many convictions."	He's got a record a mile long.
"I'm sorry we let her get away."	We should have prosecuted.
"She has a long and notable record."	The police know her well.
"He honestly felt that his previous position was too confining."	He did time in the Big House.
"It won't take long for him to break in at your place."	He's burglarized every other place he's worked.

"He's the type of man I'd want to have in a hard sell/cell situation."[5]

...and throw away the key.

---

[5]This sentence uses a homophone and works for oral recommendations. For a discussion of homophones, see pp. 101-103.

Disagreeableness

· · · ·

Recommendation	Meaning
"I am pleased to say that this candidate is a former colleague of mine."	I can't tell you how happy I am that she left our firm.
"When this very intelligent young man left our employ, we were quite hopeful he would go a long way with his skills."	We hoped he'd go as far away as possible.
"He's always trying."	He'll get on your nerves.
"You won't find many people like her."	In fact, most people can't stand her.
"One usually comes away from him with a good feeling."	He's a most unpleasant person.
"He's a difficult man to replace."	He'll sue if you try to fire him.

"You can ask him to do anything and he won't mind."

He won't do what you ask, but he won't mind your asking.

"She's one of the most discriminating people you'll ever meet."

She hates Blacks, Indians, Asians ... almost everybody.

"There's no questioning his abilities."

He gets angry if you do.

"He will take full advantage of his staff."

He even has one of them mowing his lawn after work.

"I could never give her enough credit for the job she did for us."

She always wanted more.

"He had a lot of brass pushing for his promotion."

He's got a lot of nerve.

"It was a crying shame when he left our firm."

What an ugly scene he made.

"It was a pleasure working with her for the short time that I did."

Thank God it wasn't longer.

"He takes a lot of enjoyment out of work."

... and ruins it for others too.

"Her input was always critical."

She never had a good word to say.

"The breadth/breath of the man is overwhelming and quite obvious to those who work closely with him."[6]

He's got the worst halitosis you'll ever experience.

"There's not a person in the office who could find fault with her work."

She would sulk if they did.

"How well did she get along with her fellow employees? Just let me say that most everyone here called her 'Mother.' "

She was always nagging.

"I would place this student in a class by himself."

His b.o. was that offensive.

"It's sad to see so many workers like her leaving."

They really were happy she left, though.

"In/sensitivity and in/consideration toward others — in these characteristics he was remarkable!"[7]

He didn't give a damn about others.

---

[6]This sentence uses a homophone and works for oral recommendations. For a discussion of homophones, see pp-101-103.
[7]For an explanation of the space oddity (/), see pp. 24-25.

"He enjoys a good wine/whine from time to time."[8]	What a complainer!
"There was much to - do in her division when we hired her as manager."[9]	Everyone was upset.
"I can't say anything bad about him."	I'm afraid to.
"She doesn't mind authority."	She just does what she wants.
"He works furiously whenever he faces an important deadline."	He gets very angry when he is rushed.
"The man will floor you with his ability."	He's got a great knock-out punch.
"He is a self-made man."[10]	… mainly because nobody else would help him.

---

[8] This phrase uses a homophone and works for oral recommendations. For a discussion of homophones, see pp. 101-103.
[9] The ambiguous punctuation mark used between *to* and *do* is called an "is-it-or-isn't-it hyphen."
[10] Oscar Levant often used this line.

"We were shocked when she resigned. We didn't think she would ever leave the firm."

It's about time.

"He's the type of worker who just won't quit."

... so we had to fire him.

"From the first day she began working with us, no one has shown any more interest in the firm."

She's driven away all our customers.

"Most of his staff would like to see a picture of him hanging in the president's office some day."

Actually, they wouldn't care if he were shot, drowned, or pushed out a window.

Dishonesty

· · · ·

Recommendation	Meaning
"He is the type of man who takes everything with good humor."	He'll steal the pants off you—and smile.
"Even though her work record was only average, her true ability was deceiving."	She was extremely adept at lying.
"He left us with nearly one million dollars last year."	He ran off under suspicion of larceny.
"I'm not sure why he left. There were rumors of a personality clash, and I understand he just couldn't take any more."	He took everything that wasn't nailed down.
"He is definitely a man to watch."	I don't trust him.
"You simply won't believe this woman's credentials."	She faked most of her resumé.

"Give him the opportunity and he will forge a name for himself."

Don't leave any blank checks lying around.

"She merits a close look."

Don't let her out of your sight.

"As honest as the day is long."

This phrase is best used in letters written in December, preferably on the twenty-first.

"The man is simply an unbelievable worker."

You can't trust him for a minute.

"I never knew her ₒ to be dishonest."[11]

To be honest, I knew her.

"I know him ₒ to be honest, and I know him ₒ to be frank."[12]

Yep, I know him. (This "nothing" recommendation also works well for guys named ... you guessed it.)

---

[11]For an explanation of the quomma (ₒ) and its uses, see pp. 19-22.
[12]Ibid.

Incompetence
. . . .

Recommendation	Meaning
"I most enthusiastically recommend this man with no qualifications whatsoever."	He's woefully inept.
"I understand that she would very much like to work with you if possible."	She just can't seem to get herself moving, though.
"I wouldn't hesitate to give her an unqualified recommendation."	She just doesn't have the skills for the job.
"No amount of praise would suffice for the job that he's done for us."	He's bungled everything he ever tried to do.
"Her former boss was always raving about her work."	Her mistakes nearly drove her boss mad.
"He would always ask if there was anything he could do."	We were always wondering too.

"His value to the firm is, if anything, far greater than others who have held his position."

I'm not sure if he's worth much, but the others before him were even worse.

"He has completed his schooling, and is now ready to strike out in a career."

I expect his batting average to be .000.

"We hope to find a match for the job he performed for us."

Hold the match. Maybe a shredder would be better.

"When he was here, there wasn't much work ₒ which he couldn't do."[13]

He couldn't even do small tasks.

"There was an overwhelming amount of responsibility ₒ for her."[14]

Anyone *else* could have managed it easily.

"His credentials are nothing ₒ which should be laughed at."[15]

The guy has so few qualifications that it's a joke.

"This job requires few skills ₒ which he lacks."[16]

There's almost nothing he can do.

---

[13]For an explanation of the quomma (ₒ) and its uses, see pp. 19-22.
[14]Ibid.
[15]Ibid.
[16]Ibid.

"You will soon find yourself happy to have her on board."

... a one-way bus to Peoria.

"You'll never see this man spoiled by success."

... because it's unlikely he'll ever be successful.

"I would emphasize his performance in the following areas: in/capable managerial skills, in/decisive actions, and in/correct judgments."[17]

He can't do anything right.

"She is resigning a position which she has held with our firm for many years; I truly wish there were more people like her."

... who would resign too.

"We were teetering on the threshold of bankruptcy last year, but his efforts pulled us through."

... all the way across the threshold to bankruptcy.

"We see a brilliant career ahead of her."

... far ahead of her.

---

[17]For an explanation of the space oddity (/), see pp. 24-25.

"For the services he has rendered to our firm over the years, we find ourselves deeply indebted."

In fact, because of him we're now in hock up to our ears.

"There are no - accounts that I would hesitate to put this man in charge of."[18]

He could mess up *anybody*.

"She works without direction."
   ... or ...
"How much supervision does she need? Let me say that she works ₒ well ₒ without direction."[19]

She's the most disorganized person you'll ever find.

"He wants to work for you in the worst way."

He actually takes delight in fouling things up.

"There was no limit to the credit she was given while working for us."

And now she's got every bill-collection agency in town after her.

"We wish we had ten employees like him."

Unfortunately we have twenty.

---

[18]The ambiguous punctuation mark used between *no* and *accounts* is called an "is-it-or-isn't-it-hyphen."
[19]For an explanation of the quomma (ₒ) and its uses, see pp. 19-22.

"I can't remember ever hearing a single colleague complain about her work."

They generally sent a delegation.

"The attention he devotes to details is not excessive."

... to say the least.

"We are looking for great things from him."

... but we can't find them.

Lack of
Ambition

· · · ·

Recommendation	Meaning
"Whenever I would ask her to do something quickly, it usually took a second to complete it."	… a second person, that is.
"Once she got started on a project, she wouldn't stop until it was finished."[20]	It's the only thing she actually did in all the years she was with us.
"He couldn't care less about the number of hours he had to put in."	We wish he could have cared enough to work them.
"He is not the type to run away from responsibility."	He'll walk very quickly, though.

---

[20]For a discussion of the schizocolon (⸮), see pp. 22-23.

"From the moment he arrives at work, he is raring to go."

... home.

"Whenever there is a tough task at hand, she is usually out/standing."[21]

... out standing somewhere else.

"She didn't think much of the extra time she had to work."

In fact, she didn't do much thinking during her regular work hours.

"Is he enthusiastic about working? He wants to work just so much."

... and then take a nap or maybe go home early.

"'He won't do anything ₒ which will make your firm lose money."[22]

His performance level is nil.

"His principal ambition was to get a/head in his department."[23]

He hated to have to use the washroom down the hall.

"She commands the respect of everyone with whom she works."

... but she rarely gets it.

---

[21]For an explanation of the space oddity (/), see pp. 24-25.
[22]For an explanation of the quomma (ₒ) and its uses, see pp. 19-22.
[23]For an explanation of the space oddity (/), see pp. 24-25.

"Success won't go to his head."

How could it? He's never had any.

"She just might be the best accountant your firm has ever hired."

Then again, she might not.

Laziness

· · · ·

Recommendation	Meaning
"You will be very fortunate to get this person to work for you."	She's not very industrious.
"He could not have done a better job for us if he had tried."	He's both lazy and incompetent.
"I think it's safe to say that his true interests were lying in the stockroom."	He used to sneak naps there.
"No job is too much for this man to handle."	He can't deal with any kind of work.
"She works effortlessly."	She doesn't move much.
"You will never catch him asleep on the job."	He's too crafty to get caught.
"He always found his work challenging."	It was hard for him to get going.

"She doesn't think twice about attacking a difficult problem."

In fact, she doesn't think about it at all.

"He spared no effort in his work."

He did as little as possible.

"You should seriously consider initiating an offer, since he probably won't apply himself."

He certainly didn't apply himself to anything *we* ever asked him to do.

"She always worked without a care."

If she made a mistake, so what!

"About his motivation? He is literally driven to work."

His wife drives him to the office.

"He would like nothing better than working for you."

He would rather do nothing at all.

"The volume of work which he performed was, if anything, much more than we expected."

Did he ever do anything? I really don't know.

"In her work there was nothing to complain about."

... because she did literally nothing.

"How would I describe him as a worker? Definitely over/achieving."[24]	His achieving days are long gone.
"You'll be lucky to find her type."	She wouldn't type when she worked for us.
"She never seems to have too much work to do."	... so she knits a lot.
"He won't waste any time at work."	He probably won't even show up.
"He will never do anything ₒ which will disappoint you."[25]	The guy's a lazy bum, as you'll find to your dismay.
"She has sometimes been cited/sighted at work."[26]	Once in a while she decides to come to work.
"He was never too far from the center of intellectual activity."	The farther the better thinking made his head hurt.
"I would pursue the possibility of her working for you."	There's just a *chance* she might do something.

---

[24]For an explanation of the space oddity (/), see pp. 24-25.
[25]For an explanation of the quomma (ₒ) and its uses, see pp. 19-22.
[26]This LIAR phrase uses a homophone and works for oral recommendations. For a discussion of homophones, see pp. 101-103.

"Once he put his mind to his work ﹔ nothing could stop him."[27]

Except for that one time, he was virtually worthless.

"He was with our firm a few years back, but I can't remember the exact dates he worked for us."

I think he might have shown up once or twice.

"She's not averse to working over/time."[28]

She won't mind doing it ... eventually.

"He will do nothing ₒ which will lower your high regard for him."[29]

He's definitely a loafer.

"He thinks little of hard work."

We wish he'd think more of it.

"I'm sure this man would leap at the chance to work for you."

... leap for cover.

"She's working ₒ for a change ₒ in her position."[30]

It's about time she did something.

"He works best under pressure."

... under the pressure of getting canned.

---

[27]For a discussion of the schizocolon (﹔), see pp. 22-23.
[28]For an explanation of the space oddity (/), see pp. 24-25.
[29]For an explanation of the quomma (ₒ) and its uses, see pp. 19-22.
[30]Ibid.

"The impression he conveys to others is no act."

He really *doesn't* do very much.

"He's not the type of person to simply go through the motions of looking busy at work."

He won't even do that.

"He always finds a way out of the most difficult problems."

He avoids them.

"She worked for us more or less for a year."

It was hard to tell just what she was doing.

"When he worked for us he never did anything halfway."

... although we'd have taken even that.

"Most people he works with would like to have/halve his salary."[31]

He's paid twice as much as he's worth.

---

[31]This LIAR phrase uses a homophone and works for oral recommendations. For a discussion of homophones, see pp. 101-103.

Loose Morals

· · · ·

Recommendation	Meaning
"She usually kept her affairs to herself."	… but word got around when she started wearing maternity clothes.
"It was a pleasure working under him."	… if I do say so myself.
"He will give you everything he's got on the job."	… and after 5:00 too.
"I remember him as very often laid ₒ back when I first began working with him."[32]	He's probably still at it.
"He scores well in an academic setting."	He has a lot of luck with the opposite sex.
"He's broad-minded."	He can't keep his mind off women.

---

[32]For an explanation of the quomma (ₒ) and its uses, see pp. 19-22.

"I am confident she will make out on her new job."	She made out with most of the guys at her old one.
"She's the kind of employee you can swear by."	She likes dirty jokes too.
"He wasn't at all self-conscious about everyone knowing he was getting bald/balled."[33]	In fact, he thought he was quite a stud.
"She's willing to bear/bare anything for the sake of her career."[34]	She wears very revealing clothes.
"He had good relations with his entire staff."	He seduced them all.
"Her trademark was in/decent dealings with others."[35]	She comes on to everybody.
"He loves a knotty/naughty problem."[36]	He enjoys a good scandal.

---

[33]This LIAR phrase uses a homophone and works for oral recommendations. For a discussion of homophones, see pp. 101-103.
[34]Ibid.
[35]For an explanation of the space oddity (/), see pp. 24-25.
[36]This LIAR phrase uses a homophone and works for oral recommendations. For a discussion of homophones, see pp. 101-103.

Mediocrity
· · · ·

Recommendation	Meaning
"Waste no time in making this candidate an offer of employment."	She's not worth further consideration.
"All in all, I cannot recommend this person too highly."	He has lackluster credentials.
"You can't offer this man too high a salary."	You're better off saving your money.
"I would like to say that I am extremely impressed with her abilities."	... but I can't.
"I can't give him enough credit for the job he's done for us over the years."	... not enough for you to consider hiring him.
"We were forever asking him for new ideas."	We were sick of the old ones.

"She has made immeasurable contributions to our firm."	Far too minor to be measured.
"He deserves just recognition as a member of our work force."	… not great, not even good, just recognition.
"In all the discussions we had over the years, his salary never came up."	We never gave him a raise.
"Whenever he asked us for a raise, we generally let him have it."	We tossed him right out of the office.
"She has a flair for writing."	She owns a felt-tipped pen.
"His record speaks ₒ well ₒ of him."[37]	Whom else would it speak of?
"He's a man of vision."	He can see.
"I can say nothing ₒ contrary to what you already know about him."[38]	I really have nothing to say.
"She worked ₒ well ₒ with others."[39]	Everyone at our firm worked with other employees.

[37]For an explanation of the quomma (ₒ) and its uses, see pp. 19-22.
[38]Ibid.
[39]Ibid.

"Whatever he did for us, we were pleased with him."

I still don't know just what he did.

"When this man walks through the office door in the morning, he comes to *work*."

Where else would the door lead?

"All in all, I might strongly suggest that she be thought eligible for consideration."

Talk about a nothing recommendation! This tops them all.

"He has an eye for details."

In fact, he has two of them.

"How did he manage those who worked under him? Quite fairly."

. . .not well, not badly, just fairly.

"She has a real head on her shoulders."

At least she did the last time I looked.

"The money you will invest in training her will be a well a spent."[40]

It's your money!

---

[40]Ibid.

Misfit

· · · ·

Recommendation	Meaning
"She's a woman with driving ambitions."	She's partial to 18-wheelers.
"If I were you, I wouldn't hesitate to give him sweeping responsibilities."	He can also handle a mop.
"He's a steady ɑ stable employee."[41]	He excels at cleaning the stalls and feeding the horses.
"In what position can his talents be used best? I would say the head of your departmental office."	… a born washroom attendant.
"She's excellent at taking orders."	She used to work at McDonald's, in fact.
"His enthusiasm is catching."	He always wanted to play for the Yankees.

[41]For an explanation of the quomma (ɑ) and its uses, see pp. 19-22.

"I see a brilliant career for him down the road."

... as the flagman at a highway construction site.

"As soon as you see his credentials ₒ laying bare ₒ you'll realize what an unusual work background he has."[42]

He used to work in a nudist camp.

"When I last saw her, her business was just picking up."

... litter, mostly.

---

[42]Ibid.

Stupidity

····

Recommendation	Meaning
"There is nothing you can teach a man like him."	He's hopeless.
"She could never stay away from a project too long."	We wish she would have stayed away longer.
"He is only thirty, but he has the mental faculties of a man three times his age."	He's bordering on premature senility.
"I would place his research on the cutting edge."	... of the shredder.
"She couldn't have done a better job for us."	Too bad, but she wasn't very bright.
"It seems that his potential clients always wind up giving him the business."	They always give him a hard time.

"You will find him to be among the most intelligent people you will ever meet."

He likes to hang around with smart people ... but it doesn't seem to rub off.

"He doesn't know the meaning of the word *quit*."

He can't spell it, either.

Unemployability

Recommendation	Meaning
"I can assure you that no one would be better for this job."	She is so unproductive that the position would be better left unfilled.
"After he left our firm last year, his job was to go begging for some time."	He spent his days panhandling.
"I am confident that no matter what task he undertakes, he will be fired with enthusiasm."	He won't last long on the job.
"Hire him and you'll not only get a serious man but a most educated one to boot."	… right out the door.
"We had nothing but regard for this woman."	… so we didn't hire her.

"When they made him, they threw away the mold."

It wasn't worth keeping.

"There were never too many complaints about his work."

There were lots of them and they were all justifiable.

"No salary would be too much for her."

Don't waste your money on her.

"I really cannot recall him ◦ never having done a good job for us."[43]

I'll never rehire him.

"She deserves no small part of the credit for the success of her division."

... not one iota, in fact.

"He's nobody's fool."

But if you hire him, he'll be *your* fool.

[43]For an explanation of the quomma (◦) and its uses, see pp. 19-22.

"He was a notable employee in the following ways: in/competent dealings with customers, in/articulate sales presentations, and in/considerate behavior toward his fellow employees."[44]

The guy's a zero any way you slice it.

"She is an out/going person."[45]

She won't last long.

"There's no mistaking this man's potential."

He has none.

"He was always at our disposal."

... which is exactly where you'll want to put him.

"He'll go much faster than you expect."

He's never lasted anywhere very long.

"Is she good? Let me say that *good* is not the word."

... *worthless* is, though.

---

[44]For an explanation of the space oddity (/), see pp. 24-25.
[45]Ibid.

Unreliability
. . . .

Recommendation	Meaning
"There was no end to the tasks he would undertake for us."	He never finished his assignments.
"She will readily clutch at opportunities."	She gets so nervous she falls apart.
"He would take on every task with complete abandon."	He always gave up.
"Almost nothing could keep her from her work."	She's easily distracted.
"The most insignificant detail never escaped his attention."	He labored over petty matters.
"He's a promising worker."	... promising to get it right next time, promising not to be late again, promising to stay awake at his desk ...

"It was a wonder how he ever managed ₒ putting as much time as he did into his outside interests."[46]

How could he supervise anyone? He was almost never at the office.

"As office manager, her principal concern was eliminating as much waste/waist as possible."[47]

She even did aerobics in the ladies room.

"She'll nod whenever you ask her to do something."

She has a hard time keeping her eyes open at work.

---

[46]For an explanation of the quomma (ₒ) and its uses, see pp. 19-22.
[47]This LIAR phrase uses a homophone and works for oral recommendations. For a discussion of homophones, see pp. 101-103.

Miscellany

. . . .

Recommendation	Meaning
"Stamina? He once worked three consecutive shifts before relieving himself."	How could he hold it that long?
"I am confident that he will make quite an impression wherever he decides to settle."	I can tell you that the impression his 300-pound bulk left on our sofa lasted for weeks.
"He's a striking individual."	He's not shy about putting in time on the picket line.
"The fact that she got her foot in that client's door was amazing. I would have to call her feat/feet prodigious."[48]	Size 16E, at least.

---

[48] Ibid.

"Relative to many higher-ups in our firm, this man has a great future in store for him."	He's related to the president, the vice-president, the treasurer, etc.
"He always shows a lot of Polish in his dealings with customers."[49]	He is usually munching on a kielbasa.
"You won't often see her refuse."	She is very careful about concealing her garbage.
"She would always light up whenever we gave her more responsibility."	She smoked like a fiend.
"Is he a good credit risk? Let me just say that the attention he gives to his bills is unremitting."	He owes every creditor in town.
"He's the kind of person you can lean on when you have a problem."	He usually succumbs to pressure.
"His reaction to fellow workers in need of assistance is moving."	He'll just walk away.

[49]For an explanation of capital confusion, see p. 24.

"She always has the time for her fellow workers."	She loves to show off her Rolex.
"She's a far-sighted member of our management team."	She can't see a thing without her glasses.
"If you're interested in bringing some new blood into your firm, I'd definitely make him an offer."	I suspect he's a vampire.
"At any rate, you'll find he will work hard at his job."	You can pay him anything and he'll take it.

Form Letters

....

You might think it thoughtless to use a ready-made ambiguous form letter for a recommendation. But wait a minute. Almost anyone who's ever written more than one letter of recommendation probably has borrowed words, phrases, and whole sentences from previously written letters. And why not? After spending hours on a great opening sentence, on a "just right" set of compliments, and on a punchy closing line, why reinvent the wheel with every new letter you write? Besides, everyone nowadays occasionally uses ambiguous stock phrases to describe persons, places, and things. For example, how many eulogies have you sniffled through and heard "All our lives are a little bit richer for having known the departed"? (Funny, but I usually can't recall being mentioned in the will.)

This chapter contains a sampling of form letters, each including many phrases and sentences from the lexicon in the previous chapter. Each one is preceded by a short description of the work habits, character, and traits of a hypothetical person. To use the letters, simply select the one that corresponds most closely to the person you're recommending. Okay, so the match isn't perfect. Add a few more ambiguous phrases of your own. (Be sure to mind your quommas.) Or how about adding some honest-to-goodness straight praise! What's wrong with you, anyway? Can't you say *anything* nice about a person?

·FORM LETTER A·
FOR A LAZY AND UNAMBITIOUS FELLOW EMPLOYEE

Mal Inger just called and asked you for a letter of recommendation. Taken completely by surprise, you consented. Inger used to work with you several years ago. You didn't care for him very much. He was lazy and unambitious, and left you with the lion's share of the work whenever you struggled together on a project. Afterward, however, he would take most of the credit. In fact, at one time you were so angry with him you fantasized (while watching "The Untouchables") about putting out a contract on him. But why not put out a letter of recommendation like this one instead? It's much less expensive than a contract (except, perhaps, in Chicago).

Dear _____:

I understand that Mr. Mal Inger is interested in the possibility of employment with your firm. Mal has asked me to write a letter of recommendation, and I have cheerfully consented.

I am pleased to say that Mal is a former colleague of mine. We were employed with the same firm several years ago, and worked together on several projects during that time. Once he put his mind to his work ; nothing could stop him. He would never think twice about attacking a difficult problem, and he always seemed to find a way out of it.

Mal has confided to me that he is working ₒ for a change ₒ in his job. I honestly feel that you will be very lucky to get him to work for you. And Mal? I think he would like nothing better.

Sincerely yours,

_____

·FORM LETTER B·
FOR A VERY DISAGREEABLE PERSON

Ms. Marian Haste worked as your executive secretary last year. What a sourpuss! She was always in a foul mood, never smiled, and rarely had a nice word to say to anyone. Once, when you brought her flowers during National Secretary Week, she simply scowled and said "So who died?" Since that time, you only remember her during National Pickle Week.

Some say she wasn't always as miserable as when you knew her. Rumor has it that she was happy until she married a man she had known for only a few weeks. Shortly afterward he disappeared, leaving her a note explaining that he was an alien from the planet Vulcan and had to go on a five-year mission to explore strange new worlds. (He's apparently signed up for several extra tours of duty.) Others say Marian is a Chicago Cubs fan. Unfortunately, if the latter rumor bears any truth, there is little hope for her recovery.

Marian has recently written to you and asked for a recommendation for a new job. What do you say?

Dear _____:

I understand that Ms. Marian Haste is under consideration for a job with your firm. I am pleased to say that I used to work with Ms. Haste, and I have consented to write this letter of recommendation for her.

I don't think you will find many people like Ms. Haste. Whatever work we gave her, she was always trying. Her advice, moreover, was always freely given and absolutely critical.

Most of the people who worked with Marian thought she took a lot of enjoyment out of work. Her co-workers had so much affection for her, almost everybody called her "Mother." How much has she been missed since she left? Well, recently I heard several of her former colleagues say that they would love to see a portrait of her hanging in the office where she used to work.

When Marian left our firm, it was a crying shame. It's sad to see people like her leaving. However, I sincerely hope that she will go a long way in her new career.

Sincerely,

_____

·FORM LETTER C·
FOR A
DISHONEST STUDENT

Fast Eddy Duperey was probably the most dishonest student you ever encountered. Although he had the brains to succeed in school, he partied and boogied away his four years at Watsamatta U. The word from other students is that he cheated on every exam he ever took. Sometimes he would write formulas on the soles of his shoes (he was double-jointed). Other times he would transcribe his notes on toilet paper rolls in the washroom before a test (this is *not* easy to do); then during the exam he would feign an intestinal disease and ask to be excused. After talking about Fast Eddy with other professors, you surmised that over four years he must have attended forty funerals for his grandparents, who died suddenly during final exam weeks.

Fast Eddy's academic achievements could be written on the back of a postage stamp, but now he wants to go to law school. And he's asked you, "the professor who inspired him most," to write a letter of recommendation.

You should have said "No way," you coward, but you developed a sudden case of marshmallowitis. This letter ought to bail you out.

Dear _____:

Mr. Edward Duperey has applied for admission to your College of Law. He has asked me, as a professor of his, to write a letter of recommendation for him.

I have known Mr. Duperey for three years, having first encountered him as a student in my statistics class. His grade in the course was only average; however, I would have to say his true ability is deceiving. He is definitely a young man to watch. Most of the other professors who know Ed agree that one day he will forge a name for himself.

Mr. Duperey always found his course work challenging. In fact, once he put his mind to his work ; nothing could stop him. He couldn't care less about the hours of study his courses required of him.

All in all, I cannot recommend Mr. Duperey highly enough. I would venture to say that he will do well in any law school with no qualifications whatsoever.

Sincerely yours,

_____

·FORM LETTER D·
FOR A BAD DUDE

Des Perado worked for your company last year. He hasn't a decent bone in his entire body. He always seems to be in trouble and was arrested a number of times while he worked for you. In fact, he was once allegedly observed breaking into your safe after hours, but the night watchman later came down with a sudden case of amnesia.

Mr. Perado has an arrest record a mile long— not just for the usual burglary, robbery, and arson but also for pillaging, sacking, and plundering. (You *know* this guy is bad; the last ones to commit crimes like this were the Visigoths.) Why weren't you aware of his background before you hired him? Funny how all of his letters of recommendation were very positive.

Des took an unpaid leave of absence from your firm last year. He said he'd be gone for six months (maybe less with "good behavior"). Now he has requested a letter of recommendation for a new job. Somehow you find it hard to refuse him.

Dear _____:

Mr. Des Perado has informed me that he is being considered for a position with your firm. As his former employer, I have been asked to write a letter of recommendation for him.

Mr. Perado worked for us several years ago. While he was in our employ, he was given several citations. As far as his integrity is concerned, I will simply point out that he has a long and notable record.

You will probably see that he has held quite a few jobs over the past few years and that his work record is intermittent. I am sure Mr. Perado will be the first one to tell you that many of the other places where he spent his time were too confining, and that he wanted to break out of them.

If I were you, I would not think twice about giving him a position entailing financial responsibility. In fact, during his last year with our firm, he left us with a surplus of nearly $50,000. For the job that he did, we now find ourselves deeply indebted. I'm sorry we let him get away.

Sincerely,

_____

·FORM LETTER E·
FOR AN EMPLOYEE WITH A POOR ATTENDANCE RECORD

Billy Bob Bumphus was employed with your firm for a month last year. Never in your many years of experience have you seen a man so ill-suited to work. His absentee record was ... well, a record for your firm. When he did show up, he bungled every task assigned to him. Finally, he stopped coming to work altogether. Just last week you saw him again, panhandling down by the bus terminal. Incredibly, Billy Bob said he's got a chance at a new job and asked you for a letter of recommendation. How about this one?

Dear _____:

Mr. William Robert Bumphus has asked me to write a letter of recommendation for him. I have been informed that he is under consideration for employment with your company.

Mr. Bumphus worked for us for a short time last year, but unfortunately I cannot remember the exact dates. Quite frankly, he is not your normal everyday employee, and a man like him is hard to find. In fact, after he left us, his job was to go begging for nearly a year.

When Mr. Bumphus was with our firm, there really wasn't very much work ₒ which he couldn't do. I think now that his principal interest all along was lying in the computing area. In any case, I suggest that you not hesitate to give him sweeping responsibilities. We did, and it worked out quite well.

If you would like to hear more about Mr. Bumphus, please call. All in all, I urge you to waste no time in making him an offer of employment.

Sincerely,

_____

·FORM LETTER F·
FOR AN ALCOHOLIC EMPLOYEE

John Philip Souse will imbibe anything—beer, wine, liquor, even (it is rumored) the Aqua Velva shaving lotion he keeps in his desk drawer. Like most problem drinkers, he denies he is an alcoholic, but why then does that bottle of Aqua Velva have an olive in it?

Recently you've instituted a smoking ban among your office personnel. Your action was hailed as a bold blow for the rights of nonsmokers, but you have told no one the real reason: fear of an explosion and flash fire if John Philip should happen to sneeze while lighting up.

His heavy drinking has taken its toll on his work performance, and you have had several run-ins with him over it. Now he has been giving some thought to changing employers. Here is your chance to say everything you've ever wanted to say about him ... sort of ... in a letter.

Dear _____:

Mr. John Philip Souse is, I understand, under serious consideration for a position with your firm. He has asked me, as his supervisor, to write a letter of recommendation concerning his work experience here.

John has been employed with us for the last ten years. He has a flair for writing clear reports. The number of reports he can produce in a day, while staggering, does not accurately reflect his ability, since he often finds it necessary to go through several drafts before he thinks a report sounds just right. In any case, he always seems to be loaded with work to do.

I'm not sure why John is thinking of resigning his current position. In all honesty, though, I think his real talent may be getting wasted here. If he does leave, however, I will always think of the times he spent working for us as happy hours. The impression other people have of him is invariably high.

If I can provide any further information, please do not hesitate to call.

Sincerely yours,

_____

·FORM LETTER G·
FOR A PERFECTLY AVERAGE DULL FELLOW

Norm Humdrum is giving you fits. He's asked you for a letter of recommendation, but everything about him is so *ordinary*. He's not a nerd, but he's not cool either. He had a straight C average in college, does fair-to-middling work for your company, and gets an average raise every year. His personal life? He has an average size family (1.9 children), wears a bow-tie, drives a Ford Escort, and lives in a suburb of Cleveland.

How do you write an honest recommendation that would get anyone excited about hiring this guy?

Dear _____:

Mr. Norman Humdrum is interested in being considered for employment with your firm. As Mr. Humdrum's friend and co-worker for the last several years, I am happy to write this letter.

When Norm walks into his office in the morning, he comes to *work*. In fact, he'll never fail to give you a fair day's work. He deserves—and has received—just recognition as part of our work team.

Norm is also a man of vision when it comes to seeing what has to be done. Most of his co-workers would agree with me when I say that he has a real head on his shoulders. He also has an eye for detail, and he works o well o with others.

All in all, I can say nothing o contrary to what his resumé shows. I strongly suggest that he be considered eligible for the position he is seeking. I am confident that the time and money you invest in Mr. Humdrum will be o well o spent.

Sincerely yours,

_____

·FORM LETTERS H AND I·
FOR PERSONS OF LOOSE MORAL CHARACTER

Sexual mores are more relaxed than they used to be, but don't you still find it difficult to write a letter of recommendation for a person who always has sex on the brain? Who claims to know everyone you do—in the biblical sense? Who always finds a lewd meaning in everything you say or do?

In the following pages, you will find two brief letters for persons of loose moral character—one for a John Studd, another for a Joan Vamp. (This is an equal-opportunity, affirmative-action lexicon.)

Dear _____:

Mr. John Studd is under consideration for employment with your firm. As a former co-worker, I have been requested to write a letter of recommendation for him based on my opportunity to observe him closely on the job.

Mr. Studd always had pleasant relations with those who worked under him—the secretarial staff, in particular. This is not surprising, considering how broad-minded a person he is. I think I can safely say that outside the office his distinction was in/decent dealings with business associates and friends.

If I can answer any more questions about Mr. Studd, please feel free to contact me. In any case, I am confident that he will make out on his new job.

Sincerely yours,

_____

Dear _____:

Ms. Joan Vamp is currently being considered for possible employment with your firm. I worked with Ms. Vamp several years ago and am pleased to write this letter of recommendation for her.

I remember Joan as very often laid a back when I worked with her, although she tended to keep her affairs to herself. Most of her co-workers took great pleasure in having her at work. She also had great relations, I am told, with her bosses. Most people thought of her as the type of employee you could swear by.

Joan is the kind of person who will give you everything she's got on the job. I would waste no time making her an offer. I have no doubt she will score well in your firm.

Sincerely yours,

_____

·FORM LETTER J·
FOR AN ABSOLUTE
GOOD-FOR-NOTHING

How about a letter for someone who's got no redeeming work qualities at all? He's lazy, he's disagreeable, he's shiftless, he's a screw-up, and ... he's got ring-around-the-collar. Here's a letter that will render justice to all those traits—for a Russell Mania, a man your firm fired (with gusto) several months ago.

Dear _____:

I have been told that Mr. Russell Mania is being considered for employment with your firm, and am pleased to write this letter of recommendation for him.

Mr. Mania was employed with our firm in the accounts division last year. A seasoned employee like Mr. Mania is hard to find, and we had a difficult time replacing him. You won't find many people like Mr. Mania. His fellow workers were always raving about his work. I honestly think that he could not have done a better job for us if he had tried.

Russell thinks little of hard work, and he didn't think much of the many extra hours he had to put in during our busy season, either. It seems that we could never give him too much to do.

Russell has informed me that he is ready to strike out in a new career and would like to work for you in the worst way. If you seriously consider his application, I am confident that you will find no one better for the position. And if you do hire him, I am certain that no matter what he does for you he will be fired with enthusiasm.

Sincerely yours,

_____

Telephone Recommendations

....

So now you have a stock of form letters to use for those difficult people you've had to work with over the years. That's the good news. The bad news is, many people today prefer to give (and ask for) recommendations over the telephone. It's not surprising. You can give more information about someone in a shorter period of time over the phone. Also, with the rising tide of lawsuits, fewer people are willing to offer negative comments about someone if the comments won't remain confidential. The beauty of the phone recommendation is that it leaves no trace—unless, of course, your phone is bugged.

Oral communications have still another advantage over written ones—you can use vocal tricks. For example, a pause before an affirmative reply to the question "Was he a reliable employee?" will leave the caller wondering what you really meant. Certain types of accent, inflection, and emphasis likewise can be befuddling. Compare, for example, the implication of the unaccented response to the previous question:

"I never had any problems with him." *[A solid recommendation]* with that of the accented response:

"*I* never had any problems with him." *[But others did.]*

In this chapter, I'm going to provide you with a series of hints, tips, and suggestions for preparing yourself to give ambiguous telephone recommendations. I'll use examples from the lexicon in chapter three, including homophones (homo-whats?). I will then discuss a handful (or should I say a mouthful?) of voice tricks that can be used effectively in telephone recommendations, such as pauses, gaps, and inflections. Finally, I will provide you with a set of suitably ambiguous responses to questions typically asked in telephone requests for employment recommendations.

·DODGING THE CALL·

R-r-r-ring

"Hello, this is Fred Smith with the Acme Zoetrope Corporation. I'm calling in reference to Hugo Smedley, who I understand used to work for you. Hugo has put in an application for a job with us and I'm wondering if you can spare a few moments to answer some questions about him. Your boss put me through directly to you."

What do you do first? Stall. That's right, stall. Ask if you can call back. Never give a recommendation cold—even if it's a favorable one. Pausing to collect your thoughts and plan your remarks is especially important for an ambiguous recommendation.

Your first line of defense is to have your secretary head off the call before it reaches you with the universal "I'm sorry, he's at a meeting right now." (I've always marveled at how anything gets done nowadays in the business world since it seems everyone is at a meeting virtually every moment of the day.)

If a call does get through, you'll have to give some reason for not talking. In my experience, the more befuddling the excuse, the more effectively it puts off the caller. One of my favorites goes like this: "Look, can I call you back? I'm in the middle of inverting a matrix." This usually confuses the caller, who is often too embarrassed to admit ignorance.

Esoteric excuses are still no *absolute* guarantee against a persistent caller insisting that he or she will only take a minute to ask some questions about Smedley. To guard against this possibility, you might try imitating an answering machine:

> "Hello, this is ＿＿＿＿＿＿. I'm not in the office right now but if you leave your name and number at the tone I will get back to you as soon as I can."

Then in your finest falsetto—or castrato, if you're so (un)equipped—let fly with the signal.

·PREPARING YOURSELF·

All right. Your diversion has worked and your party is going to call you back. Now you have time to compose yourself—and your responses. What next? Well, just who was Hugo Smedley? Does he deserve a good recommendation or a LIAR one? If the latter, decide what you want to say and turn immediately to your lexicon. Remember that most of the ambiguous phrases and sentences that work well in a letter will also work quite nicely in an oral recommendation. The problem, though, is that you can't always control the drift of a phone conversation. You must be prepared to answer questions with an *immediate* ambiguous response.

Here's a technique that will work wonders: flashing. No, it's not what you think. I'm talking about flash *cards*. Remember the ones you used to memorize your multiplication tables? Well, regular practice with a set of flash cards will also help you develop a quick response. LIAR flash cards are easy to make. All you have to do is put together a list of questions most commonly asked of people giving employment recommendations (those from the telephone conversation on pp. 104-107 will do). Then for each question select one or two of your favorite sentences or phrases from chapter three. Get a set of three-by-five-inch index cards and on each one put a question on one side and a response on the other, such as:

[front]

> "Does he need a lot of supervision?"

[back]

> "Well, let me just say that generally he works without any direction."

·TELEPHONE TRICKS·

You've stalled, you've studied, and you're ready for the telephone interview. Now comes the interesting part. You actually have some new techniques to use—ones that aren't in the lexicon because they can't be used in written letters of recommendation. They're oral techniques—devices I've dubbed "vocal vague-aries."

·The Pause·

First of all we have the pause, which might be called here "the pause that perplexes." Take this example:

Q. "Would you say Smedley was an honest employee?"

A. ... *[one thousand one, one thousand two]* ... "Yes."

Q. "You *would* say he was honest then?"

A. ... *[one thousand three, one thousand four]* ... "Yes."

Caution: Use the pause sparingly. If you don't, you'll come across sounding like you're not playing with a full deck.

·The Word Drag·

The word drag is a clever device that instills a bit of doubt in the mind of the listener as to whether the speaker really means what he says. Using the above example again:

Q. "Would you say Smedley was an honest employee?"

A. " ... mmmm$_m$m$_m$m$_m$m$_m$$_{yyyyy}$$_{eeeessss}$."

If you can't read the above expression—which looks like a gaggle of letters on a roller coaster ride—the dragged *yes* begins with a short high-pitched *m* sound, which immediately drops one full octave to another *m* sound, followed by a drawn-out *yes* rising on a five-note crescendo.[1] Okay—now go back and practice (but close the doors and windows so nobody hears you). Word-dragging can be used most effectively with questions requiring a yes-or-no answer.

·The Voice Gap·

Voice gapping is yet another vocal technique that can be used effectively in oral recommendations. The voice gap is nothing but a very short pause in speaking and is the oral equivalent of the quomma, the schizocolon, or the space oddity.

For example:

Q. "In what way would you say that Smedley made the biggest impact on your firm?"

A. "I would say in (voice gap) competent handling of payroll accounts."

Here the voice gap stood for a space oddity.

---

[1] If this is too confusing, the voice modulation described above for the affirmative word drag is almost identical to that used by the Big Bopper in his "H-e-l-l-o-o-o Baby."

Or to use another example:

Q. "Would you comment on how he gets along with the rest of his colleagues?"

A. "Smedley works (voice gap) well (voice gap) with others."

Here the two voice gaps have played the role of two quommas.

·The Accented Response·

Another vocal vague-ary—the accented response—has already been mentioned at the beginning of this chapter. Suppose the question were asked:

"How would you rate his learning ability?"

Compare the meaning implied by the unaccented response:

"I would say that he has remarkable learning ability." *[A very positive recommendation]*

with the meaning implied by the accented response:

"I would say that he has remarkable learning *ability.*" *[But whether he uses his ability is another matter altogether.]*

·The Bad Connection·

When you use vocal vague-aries, you run the risk of having to clarify your answer. "Just what do you mean by that?" the caller might ask. (This is a decided disadvantage of the telephone recommendation.) If you're desperate, you might try the most drastic telephone trick of all—the bad connection. Depressing the telephone button lightly several times can give the illusion of a temporary disconnection. Continuing to speak while you are depressing the button helps to heighten the effect.

You can use this trick to destroy the questioner's train of thought if he or she has asked you to clarify a response. You can also selectively delete certain syllables—or even whole words—to make a bad recommendation sound good. I'll let your imagination run here.

·Homophones·

Another great device for oral recommendations is the homophone. Most people are more familiar with the term *homonyms*—words that sound alike but are spelled differently—and kids love to see how many they can think up: *road* and *rode*, for example, *right* and *write*, and many more. The more precise term for such words, however, is *homophone*, meaning same-sounding.

How can homophones be used in intentionally ambiguous recommendations? Easily, as the following examples show. When asked how much respect an employee's co-workers have for him, you might say:

"The breadth of the man is overwhelming and quite obvious to those working closely with him."

That's quite a compliment … unless you use a homophone for breadth, which would then turn the comment into:

"The breath of the man is overwhelming and quite obvious to those working closely with him."

What's your meaning? He's got the worst halitosis you've ever run up against.

Or how about the following:

"He was sometimes cited at his former job."

This implies that the worker probably received recognition as Employee of the Month; Top Salesman, Eastern Region; or something like that. Right? But substitute a homophone for *cited* and you get:

"He was sometimes sighted at his former job."

With the homophone substitute, the statement implies that this character probably stayed home more often than he showed up for work.

Or to use one more example, in answer to the question:

"How would you describe his salary level?"

you might respond:

"I'll just say I wouldn't have minded having his salary."

Sounds like we're talking about a highly paid executive? But substitute a homophone and we get:

"I'll just say I wouldn't have minded halving his salary."

Homophonically speaking, this guy was paid twice as much as he was worth.

As you might have noted already, the lexicon in chapter three contains a generous helping of homophones. For the definitive source, however, consult James B. Hobbs's *Homophones and Homographs: An American Dictionary*.[2]

·A TELEPHONE CONVERSATION·

Let's wrap up our discussion of these tricks with an example of a telephone conversation. Many personnel management consultants suggest that a standard series of questions be asked about a job applicant. The following hypothetical telephone conversation is based on a checklist of fifteen such

---

[2]James B. Hobbs, *Homophones and Homographs: An American Dictionary*, Jefferson, N.C. and London: MacFarlane, 1986.

questions as recommended by one such consultant.[3] In response to the questions, I have selected a number of appropriate responses from the lexicon in chapter three. The double meanings—when unclear—are in brackets. I've also liberally interspersed vocal vague-aries. Here goes.

Caller: "Good morning, this is Fred Smith of Acme Zoetrope again. I hope you've finished subverting your matron. Do you have time to talk about Hugo Smedley now?"

You: "Sure, Fred. As we say in Personnel, 'Fire away.' "

Caller: "Well, first of all, what were the dates of the applicant's employment with your firm?"

You: "I remember that Hugo worked for us for a short time a couple of years ago but I don't remember the exact dates." *[How could you remember? He hardly showed up.]*

Caller: "What were the applicant's responsibilities when he worked for you?"

You: "There wasn't much (voice gap) which he couldn't do, so we gave him sweeping responsibilities."

Caller: "What level of supervision did the

---

[3]Jeffrey Davidson, "Checking References," *Law Office Economics and Management*, Vol. 27, Spring 1986, pp. 45-50.

applicant require?"

You: "He generally worked without any direction at all."

Caller: "Did the applicant work well as part of a team?"

You: "No matter what project he was involved in, his co-workers told me that his input was always critical. Also, they felt that he deserved no small part of the credit for his team's overall success."

Caller: "Were there any work conflicts involving the applicant?"

You: "Most of the employees I spoke to said that they were happy working with him for the short time that they did. I was also told that I wouldn't find too many other workers like him."

Caller: "Was the applicant's record of attendance a good one?"

You: "*Good* is hardly the word. A man like Smedley is extremely hard to find."

Caller: "Can you point out some of the applicant's major strengths?"

You: "I can mention several ways in which he stood out among other workers: in (voice gap) accurate reports, in (voice gap) capable han-

dling of accounts, and in (voice gap) consider-
ate behavior toward his fellow staffers."

Caller: "Can you mention any weaknesses or
shortcomings of the applicant?"

You: "I really can't say anything critical about
him. *[I'm afraid of getting sued.]* But I will say
that his principal interest seemed to be lying in
the computer room, and I think his real talent
was getting wasted at work."

Caller: "Does the applicant possess adequate
learning ability?"

You: "His capacity for learning is actually
nothing (voice gap) which should be laughed
at. We soon learned that no job was too much
for this man to handle."

Caller: "How does the applicant's record compare to those of others with similar duties and
responsibilities?"

You: "Let me assure you that no one would
have been better for the job."

Caller: "Why did the applicant leave your
firm?"

You: "He was ready to strike out in a new
career. The last time we spoke about it I saw
that he was fired with enthusiasm."

Caller: "How did you replace the applicant

after he left?"

You: "After he left, his job was to go begging. I'm inclined to believe now that no one will ever replace him."

Caller: "What was the salary earned by the applicant when he was with your firm?"

You: "Without getting too much into specifics, just let me say that I wouldn't have minded halving his salary."

Caller: "Given your experience with the applicant and knowing his qualifications, would you hire him again?"

You: "I wouldn't think twice about hiring this man again. He has my unqualified endorsement."

Caller: "Thank you very much for your time. You've given me a lot of solid information about Mr. Smedley. It sounds like you lost a very capable employee when he left."

You: "You'll be lucky to get him to work for you."

AFTERWORD

If you've read this far, you're well on the road to mastering the craft of providing ambiguous recommendations.

What advantages will you enjoy? Well first of all, you'll never again have fits of anxiety about giving a recommendation for someone who couldn't hold down a job if it weighed a ton. You'll sleep better at night and probably be an all-around nicer person to live with. Also, once your prowess becomes known, you'll probably never be asked to write another recommendation. This alone is worth the price of the book.[1]

Finally, on a more aesthetic note, you will soon gain an awareness—an appreciation, even—of the fact that the world is full of ambiguous language. For example, my house-hunting friends Jean and Tom tell me that when they pick up the classified ads of the newspaper, they often read of a house that "won't last long." *[They wonder if it's safe to go inside.]* My handball partner Dan tells me about the special on "half baked chicken" at a delicatessen he frequents. *[There's no accounting for taste!]* The favorite advertising slogan of a carpet outlet in my area is "No sale beats wholesale." *[Are they trying to turn customers away?]* And if you ever visit England and try to find a carry-out restaurant, just look for a sign saying "Food to take away." *[Is British food really that bad?]*

And so it goes....

---

[1]To make absolutely certain that word gets around, I respectfully suggest that you purchase several hundred copies of this book and distribute them to your friends and acquaintances.